ADOPTION: A GREAT OPTION!

CHINA

恩典

by Carla D'Addesi and Jocelyn Hoffman

Illustrated by Haylee Scarborough

Adoption, a Great Option:
China

by
Carla D'Addesi and Jocelyn Hoffman

Library of Congress Number: 2013952192
International Standard Book Number: 978-1-60126-403-9

Printed 2013 by
Masthof Press
219 Mill Road
Morgantown, PA 19543-9516

Dedication

This book is dedicated
to the 573,000 (and counting) children
currently living in Chinese orphanages.

恩
典

Acknowledgements

We would like to thank our husbands and children who inspire us to live for Christ each day!

- Jocelyn and Carla

It was Sunday, November 29th

in the United States of America.
The Desman family was talking about the
missionary they heard in church that morning.
"Mom," said Nathan, "I felt really sad when the missionary
told us about the orphans living in China."
Mom replied, "It's heartbreaking to hear that families
in China are only allowed to have one child."
Dad added "It just isn't fair."
Nathan sighed, "I wish there was something we could do."
"Me too," Mom agreed. Something special began to stir
in her heart, "me too."

On the very same day in China . . .

There lived a fine young woman named Mei. Mei was happy because she was going to have a baby. She smiled when that sweet baby moved in her tummy. She loved that baby from the moment she knew she was pregnant.

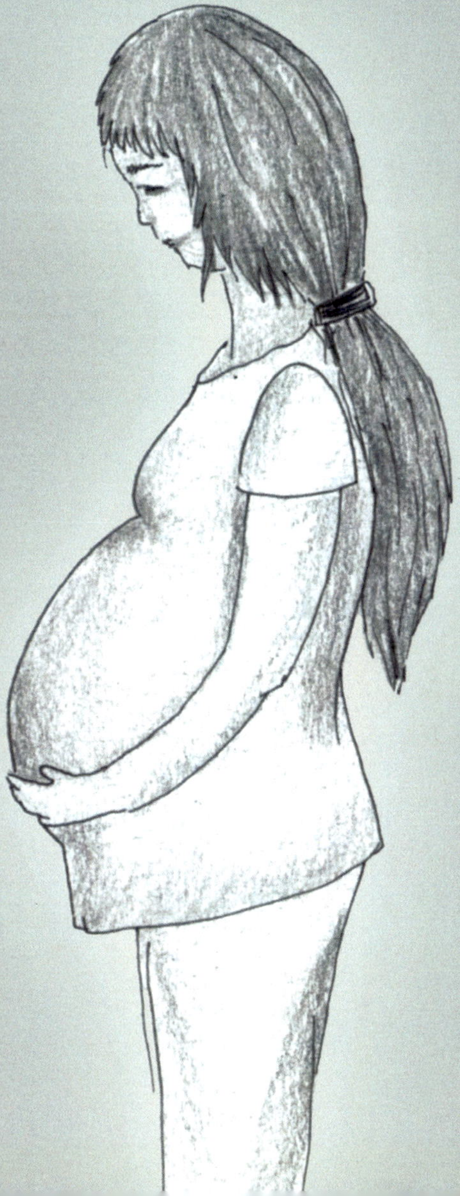

It was February 22nd in the USA.

Mom giggled as she watched her little boy playing in the snow. She began to daydream of one day having a little girl. A little girl that would help her bake cookies and wear dresses and bows. Something special was stirring in her heart again. She recalled the missionary's words spoken in church.

That's when the Lord gave her the desire to adopt a little girl. A little girl from China!

On the very same day in China . . .

Mei gave birth to a baby girl.

"I will call her Zhong," Mei thought.

"This name means she is beautiful on the inside."

Mei smiled because she knew this baby was special.

Mei loved
Zhong
very much.

It was March 4th in the USA.

Mom leafed through an adoption magazine, which had pictures of children waiting for their forever families.

"I wish this little girl could come live with us," Nathan exclaimed. "It would be fun to have a little sister!" Mom and Dad looked at each other and smiled. Mom told Dad about her desire to adopt. To her surprise, he shared that God had placed the same desire in his heart.

"Why don't you call some local adoption agencies and find out more information," Dad recommended.

On the very same day in China . . .

Mei was crying because of China's One Child Policy. Keeping baby Zhong would mean that she and her husband could lose their jobs, her son would be persecuted at school, and they would have to pay a hefty fine. Mei was distraught at being forced to give up her baby.

It was May 1st in the USA.

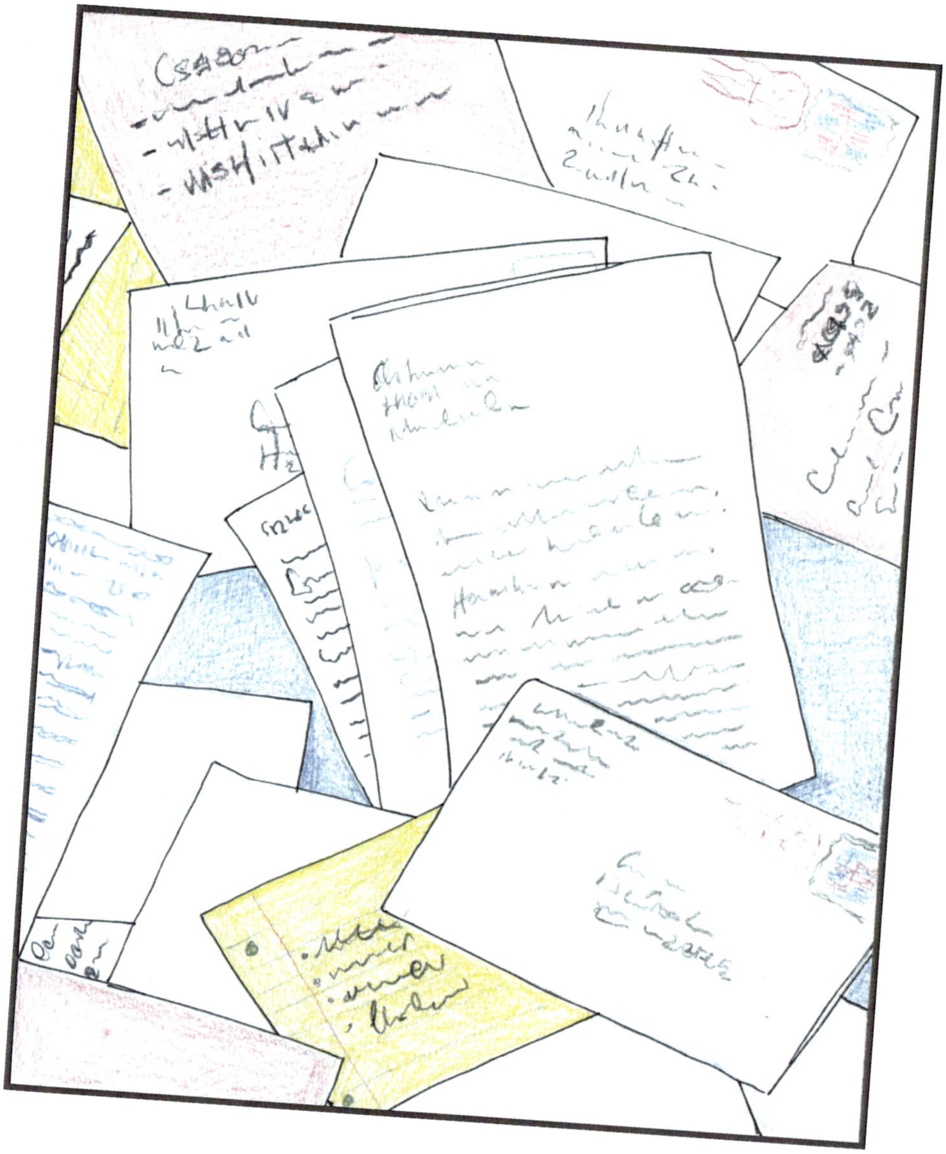

Mom had gathered lots of adoption materials and attended information meetings. She knew the process would take a long time and there would be lots of paperwork.

The Desman family continued to pray for God's guidance as they pursued their search for a little girl to join their family.

On the very same day in China . . .

Mei sobbed. She wrapped little Zhong in a warm blanket to which she pinned a very special locket. Inside the locket she wrote "Give love and a home to this gift." She placed her by the orphanage gates. Mei gave Zhong one last kiss and slipped away for fear of being caught. She knew that in China, a mother could spend the rest of her life in prison for abandoning a child. Mei kept watch over Zhong until one of the orphanage nannies took the baby safely inside.

It was June 1st in the USA.

After much prayer, the Desman family
knew they were ready to adopt.
They met with a social worker and leafed through pictures
of children who needed forever families.

How could they possibly choose one child out of so many?

As Mom and Dad turned to the last page in the big book, there she was!
It was their daughter. They couldn't explain it, they just knew.
It was at this moment they realized they needed
that little girl more than she needed them.

On the very same day in China . . .

Zhong felt lonely
in her new surroundings.

She longed to be
cuddled
and loved
by her mother.

It was August 5th in the USA.

Mom had filled out mounds and mounds of paperwork.
Mom and Dad had written an autobiography,
had their fingers printed and completed a home study.
Finally, everything they needed to do was finished.

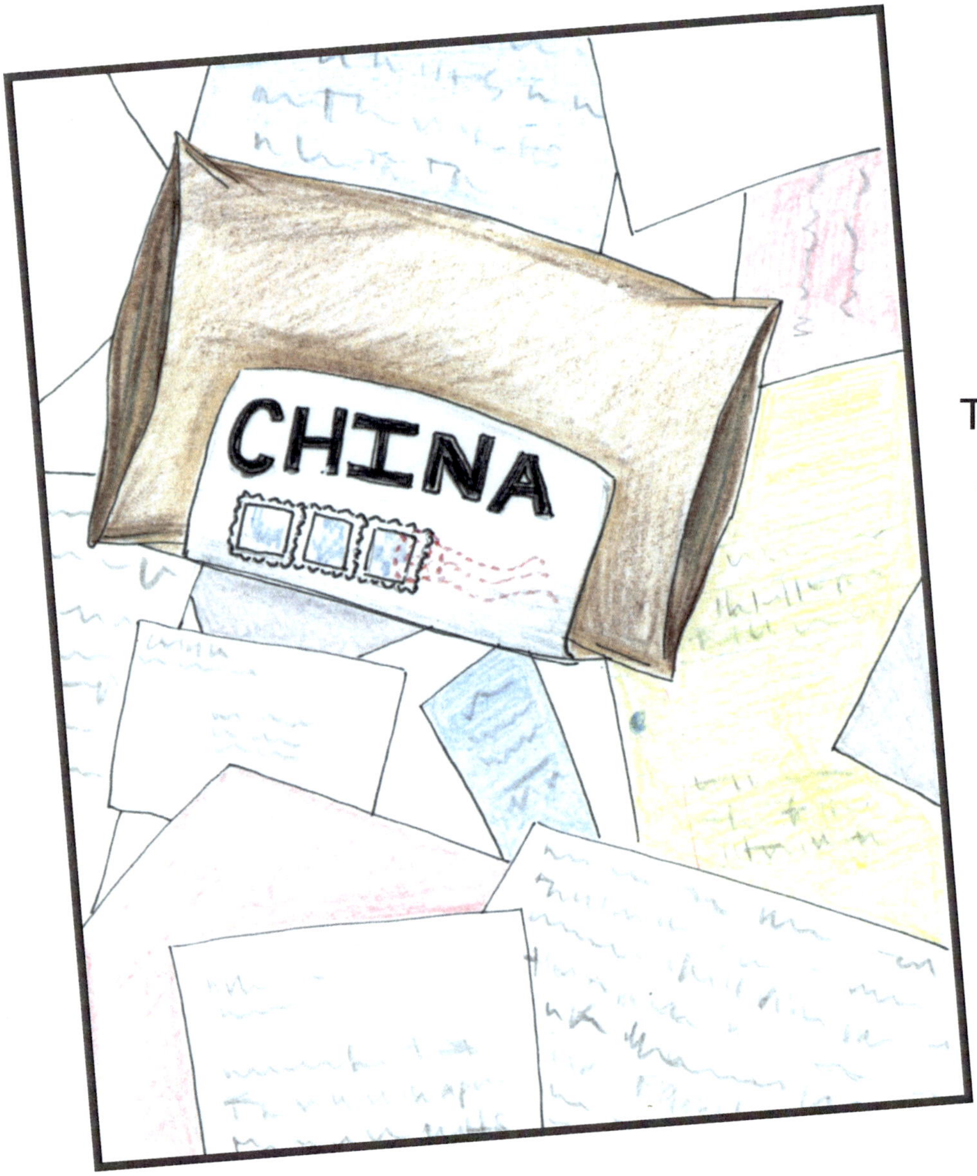

The papers were all put together in a package called a *dossier* and mailed to China.

On the very same day in China . . .

Zhong got her first tooth.
She continued to grow.
She even began to crawl.

The orphanage nannies taught her to
say "mama" and "dada."
The whole time, Zhong wore the special locket
that was given to her by her birthmother.

It was December 1st in the USA.

The Desman family anxiously waited for their
Letter of Acceptance (LOA).
"Mom," Nathan stated,
"the only gift I want for Christmas
is my baby sister."

Mom winked at Nathan
and gave him a
reassuring pat on his head.

On the very same day in China . . .

The Desman family's dossier arrived at the China Center of Adoption Affairs (CCAA). The CCAA looked over all of the documents, drafted the Letter of Acceptance, and mailed it back to the USA.

All the while, Zhong, still wearing her locket, continued to grow. In fact, Zhong was able to stand as she held on to a bed.

It was February 22nd in the USA.

There was a knock at the door of the Desman home.
Mom opened the door and was delighted to see a man holding a large white envelope. “Thank you,” Mom said.
She called Dad and Nathan into the kitchen and together they opened the package.
It was the LOA!

“Let’s celebrate!” declared Mom.

“Hooray!” cheered Nathan.

“I’ll get the ice cream,” Dad exclaimed.

On the very same day in China . . .

Zhong quietly turned one.

There were no candles,
no cake,
and no birthday gifts.

It was March 19th in the USA.

Immigration paperwork was finally completed
and the Desman family received their
Travel Approval (TA) letter from China.
They made their Swearing-In Appointment
with the consulate and began making
travel arrangements to bring their little girl home.

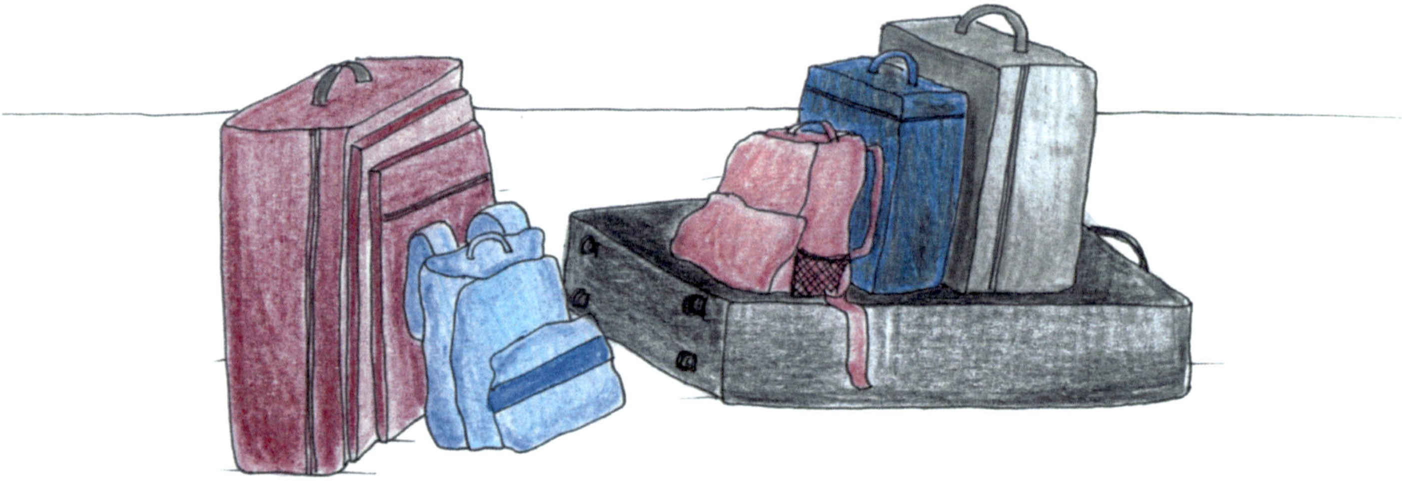

They were excited but had concerns.
Would she like their family?
Would they love her as much as they love Nathan?
They continued to pray and began to pack their belongings.

On the very same day in China . . .

Zhong took her first steps.

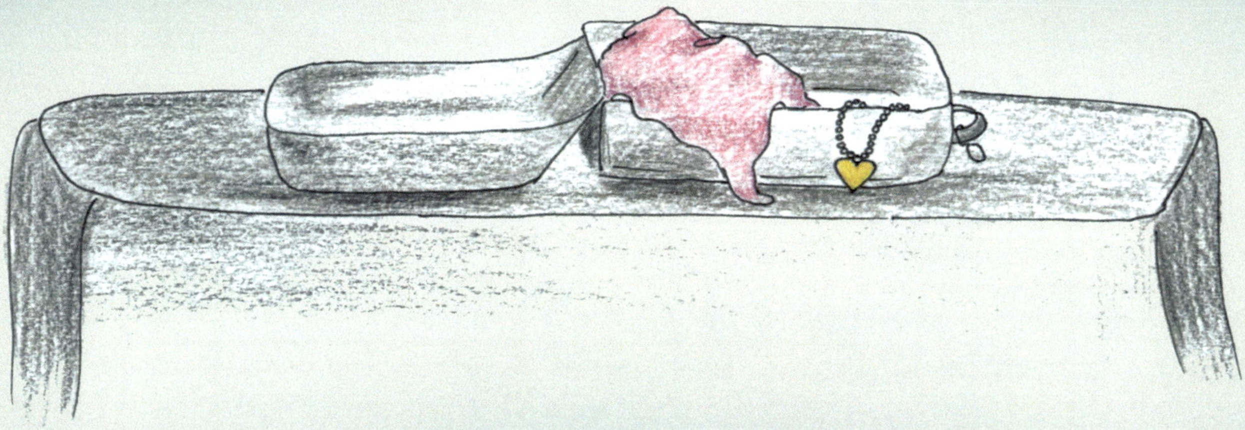

The orphanage nannies began to
prepare Zhong
for the arrival of her
forever family.
They packed
her few belongings.

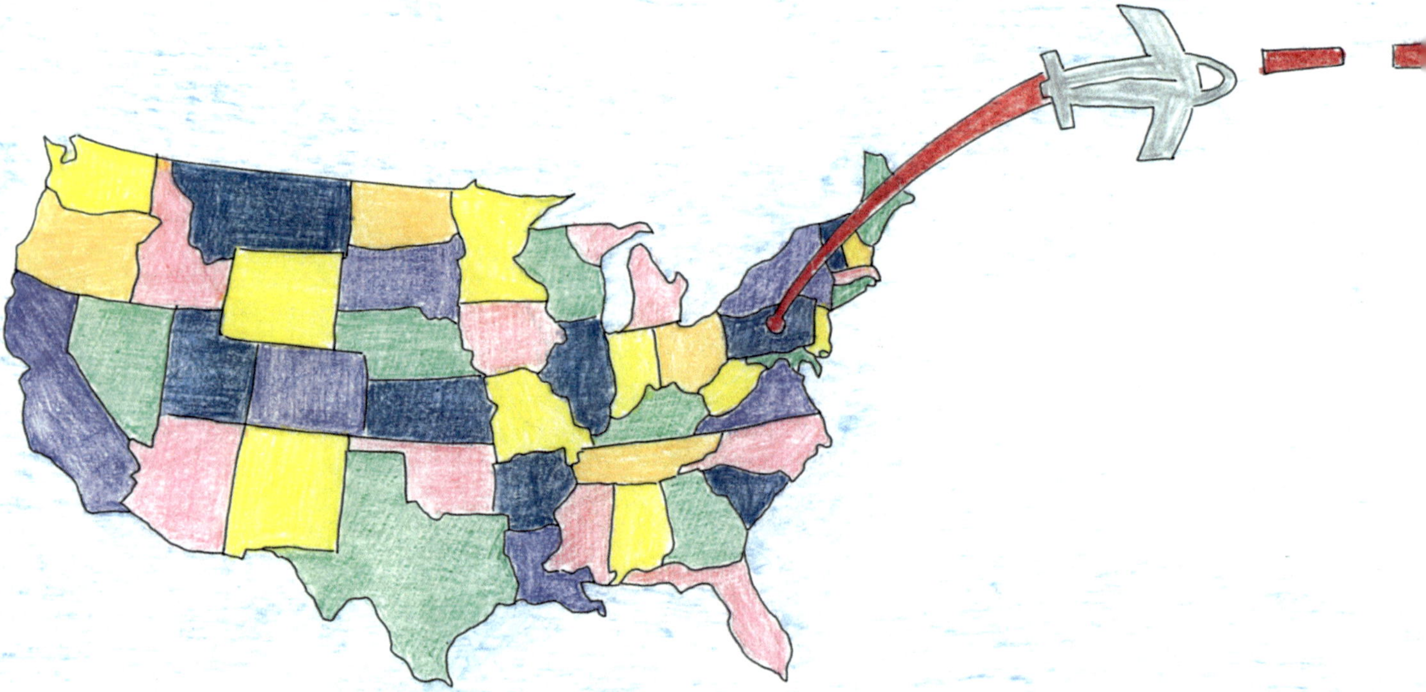

It was March 30th in China . . .

The Desman family exited the airplane and gathered all of their luggage.

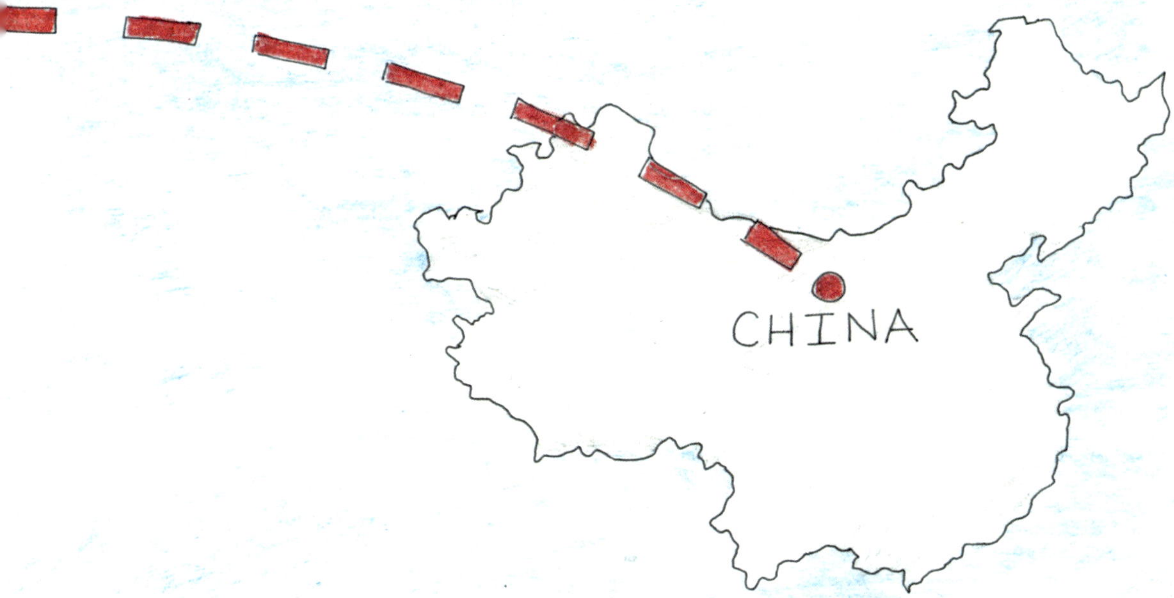

They found their tour guide and spent the next two days touring China. Although they enjoyed the culture, they *longed* to meet their little girl!

It was April 2nd!

Gotcha Day! The day for which they had been waiting! The Desman family anxiously waited in the crowded and noisy orphanage lobby, along with other adoptive parents. Every time the door opened, the room grew quiet as each set of adoptive parents expected their little girl to be brought through the door.

Finally!

Their daughter, wearing her locket, timidly entered the room. Everyone else seemed to disappear. They prayed for this child for so many months. This moment felt like a dream.

"Hi Zhong, I'm your mommy,"
Mom cooed.
"I'm your daddy,"
Dad smiled.

Both were concerned because Zhong did not respond the way they had hoped. Nathan was so happy. He wasn't sure if he should burst into tears or giggles. He chose giggles!

It wasn't until he hugged her, that she finally let go of the nanny's hand. "I'm your big brother!" he said with a grin as he handed her a lollipop. A smile appeared on Zhong's face.

It was April 10th in China . . .

After signing the final papers with a red fingerprint, and passing medical exams, Zhong was finally their little girl. Their family was complete! The Desman family boarded their flight home. They could not wait to set foot on American soil because that's when Zhong would officially become a United States citizen.

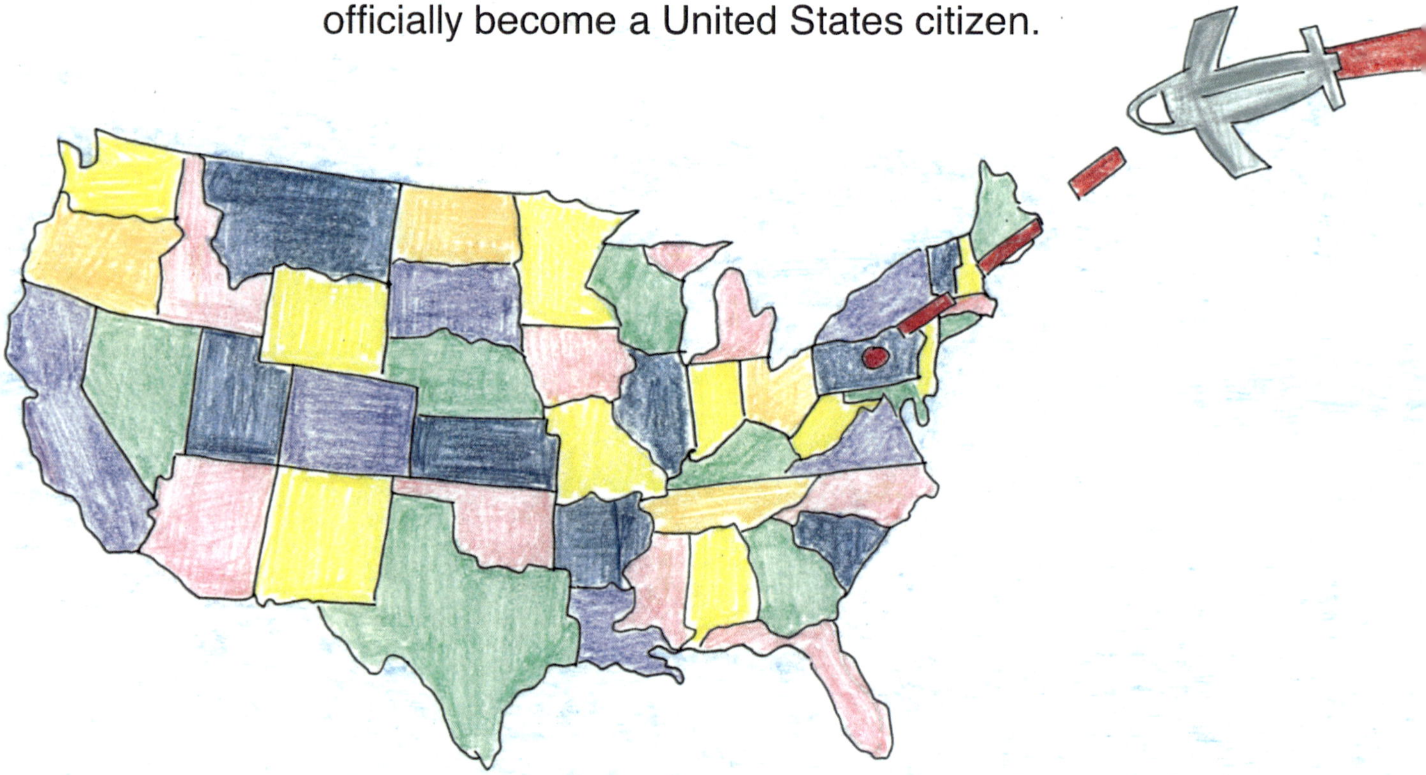

During the flight, Dad and Mom decided that Zhong's new name would be Grace which means "undeserved gift." "Grace's birthmother will never understand the gift she has given to us," Dad declared. All Mom could do was smile.

On the very same day in China . . .

Mei knew in her heart that Zhong had found the gift of love and a home.

All she could do was smile.

However, Mei never understood that it was the Desman family

who received the greatest gift of all . . .

their little girl, Grace.

Did You Know . . .
That You Can Be Adopted Too?

The Bible holds the greatest adoption story ever! As sinners, we are all separated from God, our Heavenly Father (Isaiah 59:2). However, God loves us so much that He longs for us to be His children (John 3:16-17). It is only through Jesus' death on the cross and resurrection that we gain the right to become His children (John 1:12-13). He adopts us! He calls us His own and rescues us from a life apart from Him.

Won't you consider joining the family of God? He chose you and now you have the privilege to choose Him. If you confess with your mouth that Jesus is Lord, and believe in your heart that God raised Him from the dead you will be saved (Romans 10:9). And by saved, we mean you get to spend eternity with God and your forever family! How great is the love which the Father has lavished on us that we should be called sons of God, and that is what we are (1 John 3:1)!

Share your adoption story.
Find us on Facebook
www.facebook.com/adoptionagreatoption

Adoption Lingo

Birthmother: Biological or genetic mother of a child.

China Center of Adoption Affairs (CCAA): A Chinese government organization responsible for the welfare of children in the care of orphanages, domestic adoptions, and international adoptions. (The CCAA's name has recently been changed to The China Center for Children's Welfare and Adoption. However, it is still commonly known as and referred to as the CCAA.)

Dossier: A collection or file of documents on the same subject, especially a complete file containing detailed information about a person or topic.

Forever Family: A basic social unit consisting of parents and their children without ever ending.

Gotcha Day: The day that an adopted child is placed into the family's life for adoption, in other words, the day the family "Gotcha."

Home Study: A series of interviews and home visits, along with a collection of documents and references that are part of the required pre-adoption process for all adoptive families.

Letter of Acceptance (LOA): Official approval from the CCAA to adopt your specific child. It takes anywhere from 2-4 months to receive an LOA. This letter comes after your dossier has been logged in and accepted by CCAA.

Social Worker: A person whose work is directed towards the betterment of the community and the welfare of children.

Travel Approval (TA): Permission from the CCAA to travel to China and complete the adoption of your child.

China's One Child Policy

The One Child Policy is the population control law of the People's Republic of China. It restricts urban couples to only one child. This policy was created by the Chinese government to alleviate social, economic, and environmental problems in China. The policy is controversial both within and outside China because of the manner in which the policy has been implemented, and because of negative social consequences. The policy has caused forced abortions, female infanticide, abandoned female and special needs babies and underreporting of female births.

The policy is mainly enforced through fines. Families are fined and the size of the fine depends on the family's income. The fines are significant and not just a slap on the wrist for families on a normal income. Families can lose workplace bonuses. They may also be denied promotions and risk losing their jobs. Families unable to pay their fine jeopardize having their properties seized by the government. It is well known that government officials and especially wealthy individuals have often been able to violate the policy in spite of fines. Additional penalties include forced abortion, forced sterilization, and loss of education. Families who have more than one child must pay for their children's education. While one-child families are offered free education.

About the Authors

Carla D'Addesi and Jocelyn Hoffman have been lifelong friends. They both have friends who adopted children from China. Carla and Jocelyn co-chair Bethany Christian Services' largest fundraising event in Pennsylvania; the silent auction and banquet. After serving Bethany for a number of years and hearing many heartwarming adoption stories, the Lord inspired them to write this book, in order to educate and inspire families. Carla and her husband had the privilege of serving on Bethany's board for many years. This is Carla D'Addesi's second book. The first being *Julia Learns How to Vote Wisely*. Find out more at: www.julialearns.com

About the Illustrator

Haylee Scarborough is a young artist from Maryland. She has had a love for art from a very young age. Advanced art classes in high school taught her to develop her natural God-given talent for bringing images to life, and as a senior in high school, she placed first in the Congressional Art Competition. Her artwork was then displayed in the United States Capitol building for the next year.

Haylee currently attends Bob Jones University in Greenville, SC. In her time there, she has been blessed with many opportunities to express her passion for art. She is delighted to use her gifts to teach young people about such an important cause by bringing Grace and her family to life.

References

www.theguardian.com

www.chinatravelgo.com

www.kimclement.com

www.wikipedia.org